W9-ACV-340

UNCHARTED: STORIES OF SURVIVAL

LIGHTNING STRIKE Survivor!

by Harriet McGregor

Illustrations by Alan Brown and Diego Viasberg

BEARPORT PUBLISHING

Minneapolis, Minnesota

BEAR CLAW

Credits: 21, © Yordan Nedialkov/Shutterstock; 22–23, © Vasin Lee/Shutterstock.

Supervising Editor: Allison Juda
Editor: Sarah Eason
Proofreader: Jennifer Sanderson
Designer: Paul Myerscough

DISCLAIMER: This graphic story is a dramatization based on true events. It is intended to give the reader a sense of the narrative rather than a presentation of actual details as they occurred.

Library of Congress Cataloging-in-Publication Data

Names: McGregor, Harriet, author. | Viasberg, Diego, 1981– illustrator. |
  Brown, Alan (Illustrator), illustrator.
Title: Lightning strike survivor! / by Harriet McGregor ; Illustrations by
  Diego Viasberg, Alan Brown.
Description: Bear claw edition. | Minneapolis, Minnesota : Bearport
  Publishing, [2021] | Series: Uncharted: stories of survival | Includes
  bibliographical references and index.
Identifiers: LCCN 2020008645 (print) | LCCN 2020008646 (ebook) | ISBN
  9781647470340 (library binding) | ISBN 9781647470418 (paperback) | ISBN
  9781647470487 (ebook)
Subjects: LCSH: Lightning–Juvenile literature. | Lightning–Comic books,
  strips, etc. | Mountaineering–Juvenile literature. | Graphic novels. |
  Grand Teton National Park (Wyo.)
Classification: LCC QC966.5 .M34 2021 (print) | LCC QC966.5 (ebook) | DDC
  363.34/9254–dc23
LC record available at https://lccn.loc.gov/2020008645
LC ebook record available at https://lccn.loc.gov/2020008646

For more information, write to Bearport Publishing, 5357 Penn Avenue South, Minneapolis, MN 55419. Printed in the United States of America.

CONTENTS

Chapter 1

A MOUNTAINTOP STRIKE

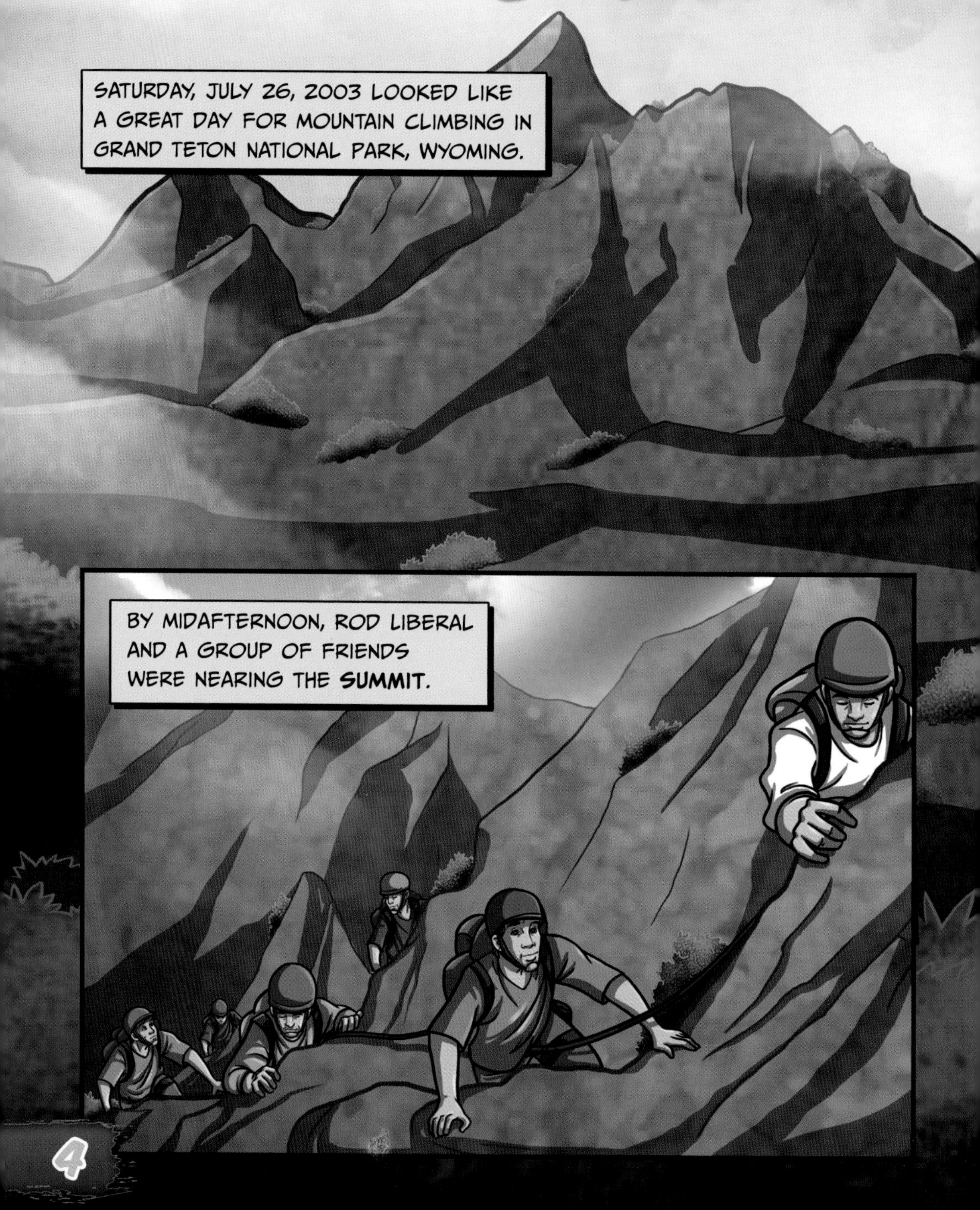
SATURDAY, JULY 26, 2003 LOOKED LIKE A GREAT DAY FOR MOUNTAIN CLIMBING IN GRAND TETON NATIONAL PARK, WYOMING.
BY MIDAFTERNOON, ROD LIBERAL AND A GROUP OF FRIENDS WERE NEARING THE SUMMIT.

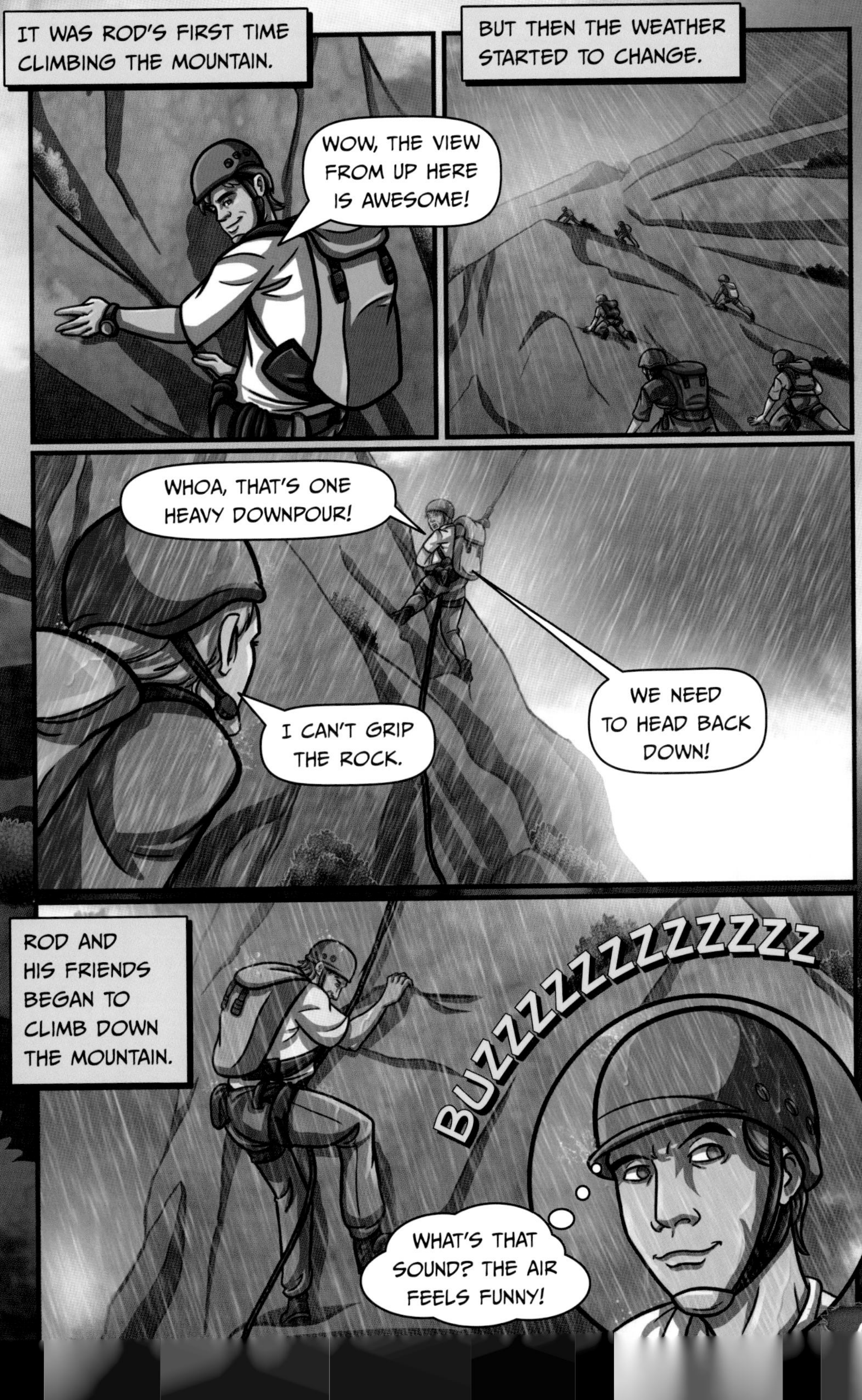
IT WAS ROD'S FIRST TIME CLIMBING THE MOUNTAIN.
WOW, THE VIEW FROM UP HERE IS AWESOME!
BUT THEN THE WEATHER STARTED TO CHANGE.
WHOA, THAT'S ONE HEAVY DOWNPOUR!
I CAN'T GRIP THE ROCK.
WE NEED TO HEAD BACK DOWN!
ROD AND HIS FRIENDS BEGAN TO CLIMB DOWN THE MOUNTAIN.
BUZZZZZZZZZZZZZ
WHAT'S THAT SOUND? THE AIR FEELS FUNNY!

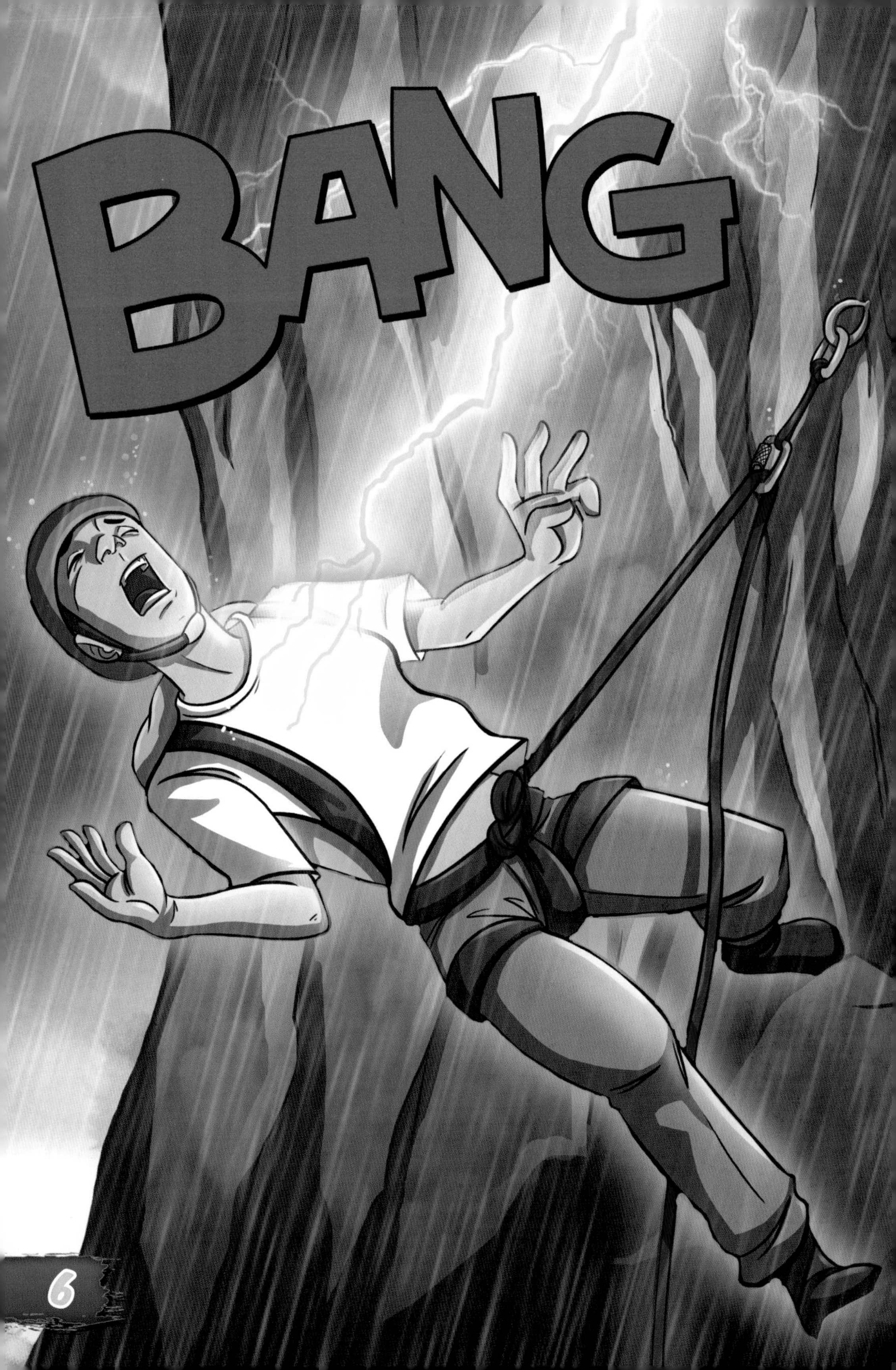
BANG

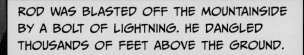

ROD WAS BLASTED OFF THE MOUNTAINSIDE
BY A BOLT OF LIGHTNING. HE DANGLED
THOUSANDS OF FEET ABOVE THE GROUND.

Chapter 2

RESCUE IN THE SKY

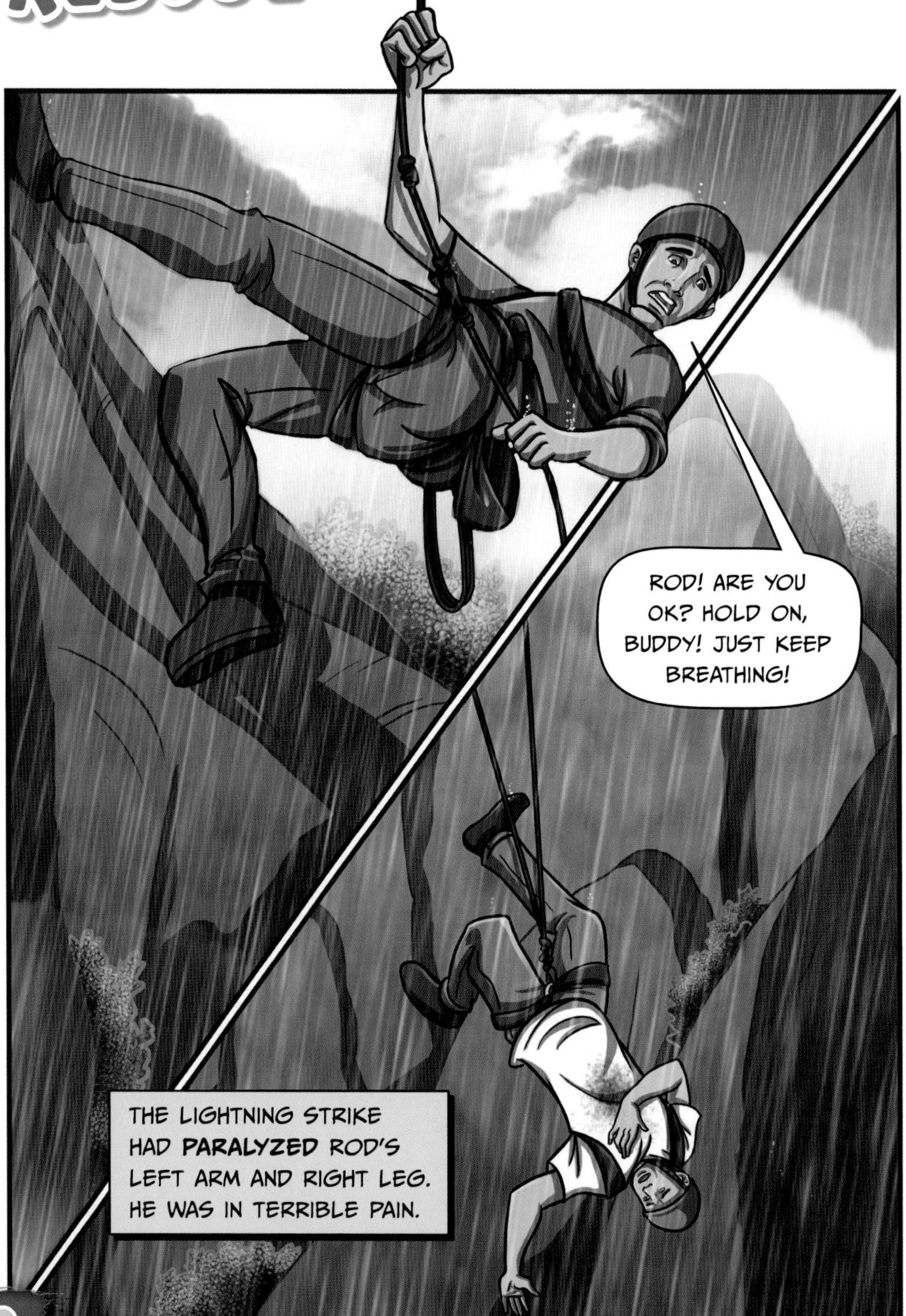
ROD! ARE YOU OK? HOLD ON, BUDDY! JUST KEEP BREATHING!
THE LIGHTNING STRIKE HAD **PARALYZED** ROD'S LEFT ARM AND RIGHT LEG. HE WAS IN TERRIBLE PAIN.

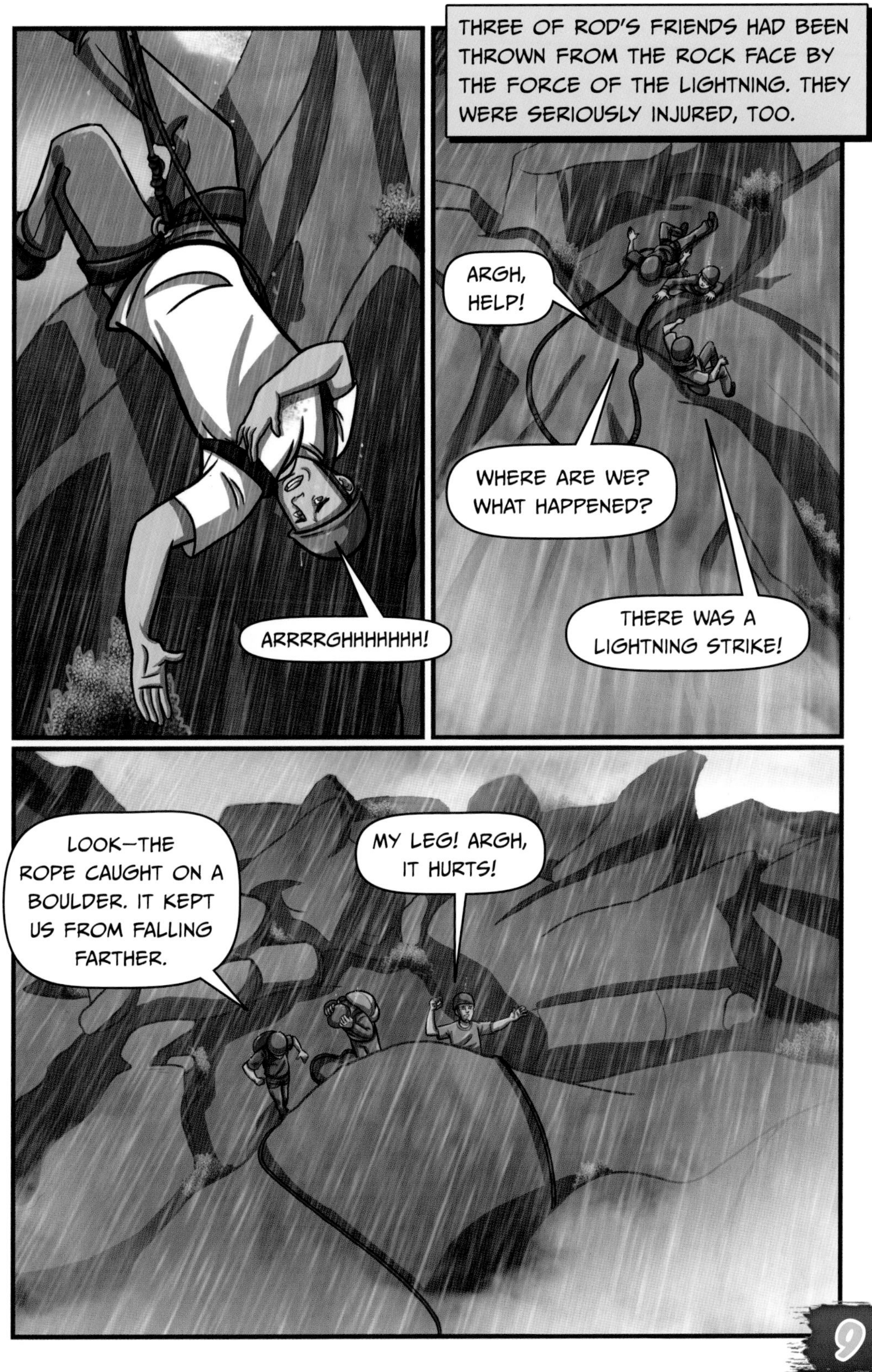
ARRRRGHHHHHHH!
THREE OF ROD'S FRIENDS HAD BEEN THROWN FROM THE ROCK FACE BY THE FORCE OF THE LIGHTNING. THEY WERE SERIOUSLY INJURED, TOO.
ARGH, HELP!
WHERE ARE WE? WHAT HAPPENED?
THERE WAS A LIGHTNING STRIKE!
LOOK—THE ROPE CAUGHT ON A BOULDER. IT KEPT US FROM FALLING FARTHER.
MY LEG! ARGH, IT HURTS!

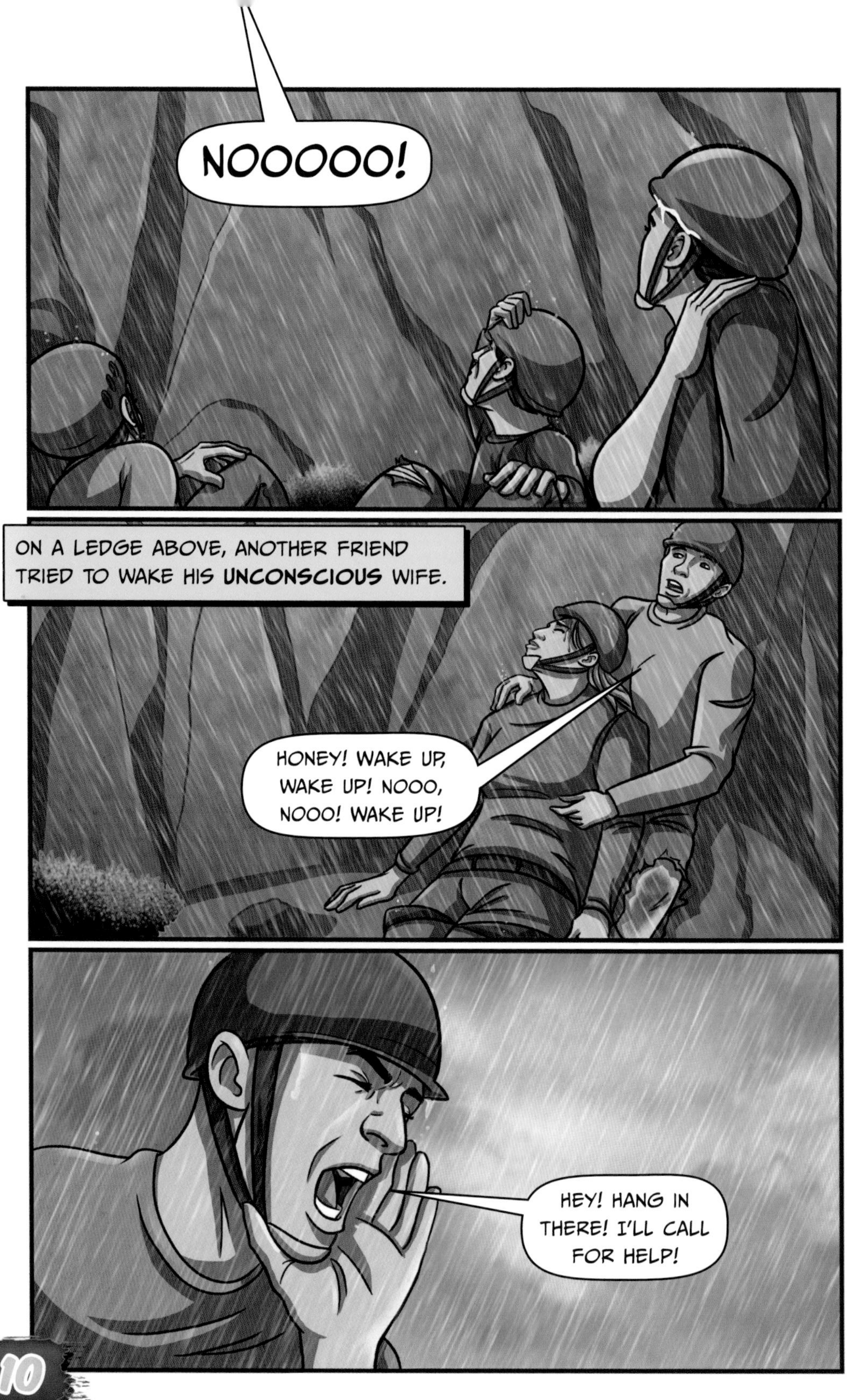
NOOOOO!
ON A LEDGE ABOVE, ANOTHER FRIEND TRIED TO WAKE HIS **UNCONSCIOUS** WIFE.
HONEY! WAKE UP, WAKE UP! NOOO, NOOO! WAKE UP!
HEY! HANG IN THERE! I'LL CALL FOR HELP!

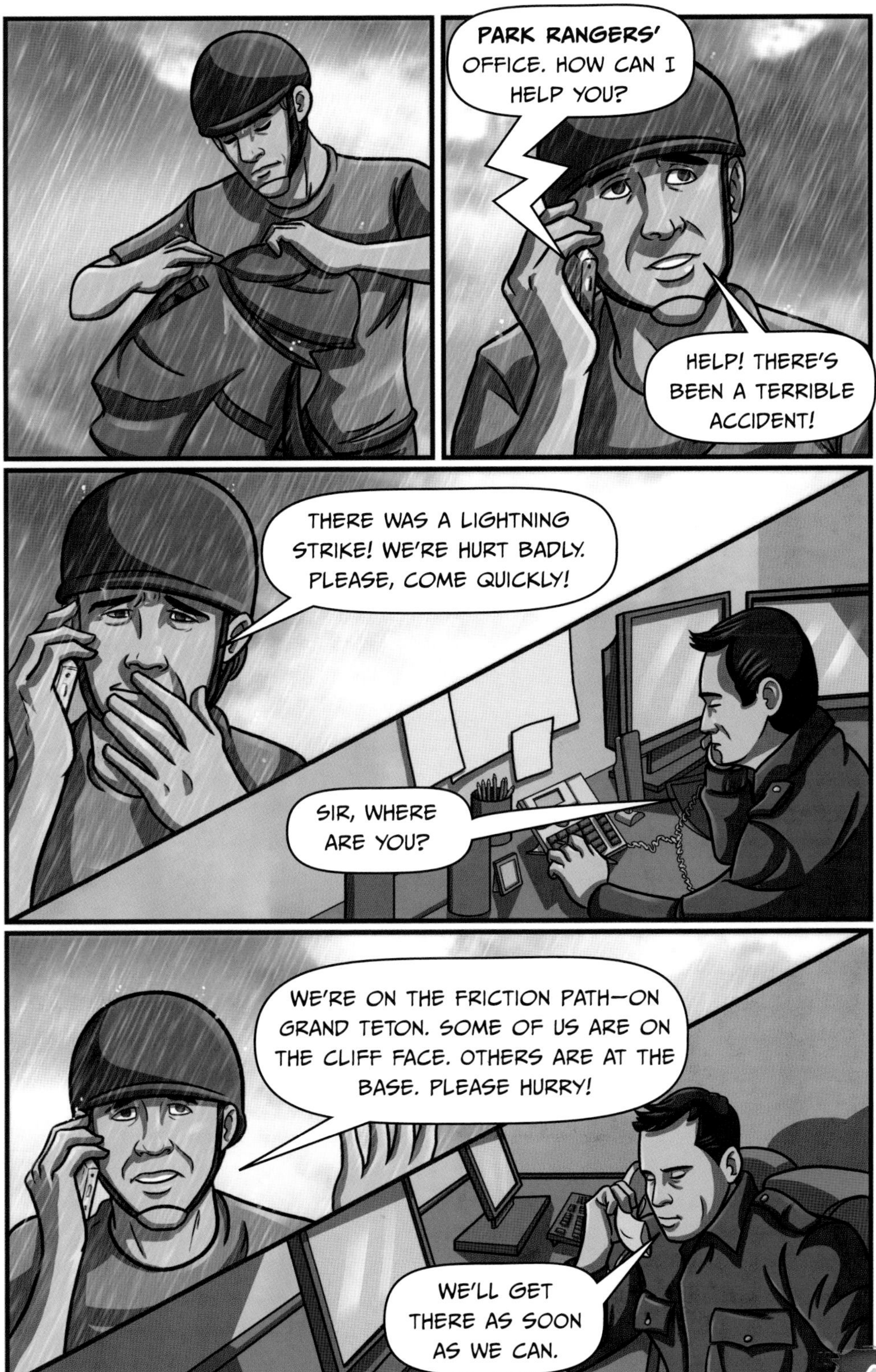
PARK RANGERS' OFFICE. HOW CAN I HELP YOU?
HELP! THERE'S BEEN A TERRIBLE ACCIDENT!
THERE WAS A LIGHTNING STRIKE! WE'RE HURT BADLY. PLEASE, COME QUICKLY!
SIR, WHERE ARE YOU?
WE'RE ON THE FRICTION PATH—ON GRAND TETON. SOME OF US ARE ON THE CLIFF FACE. OTHERS ARE AT THE BASE. PLEASE HURRY!
WE'LL GET THERE AS SOON AS WE CAN.

RANGER BRANDON TORRES QUICKLY SET UP A RESCUE MISSION.

A GROUP OF CLIMBERS HAVE BEEN HIT BY LIGHTNING. THEY'RE STRANDED 13,000 FEET* UP THE MOUNTAIN.

WE NEED RESCUE AND MEDICAL HELICOPTERS IN THE AIR RIGHT AWAY! WE HAVE TO GET THERE BEFORE DARK.

*3,962 M

LOOK FOR A PLACE TO LAND.

SET DOWN THERE, BELOW THE CLIMBERS.

HELP! HEY, DOWN HERE!!

SOME OF THE HELICOPTERS LANDED. THESE RESCUERS WOULD TRY TO REACH THE CLIMBERS FROM BELOW.

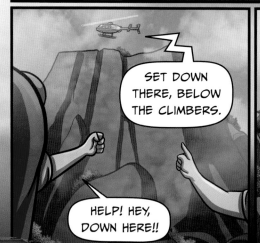

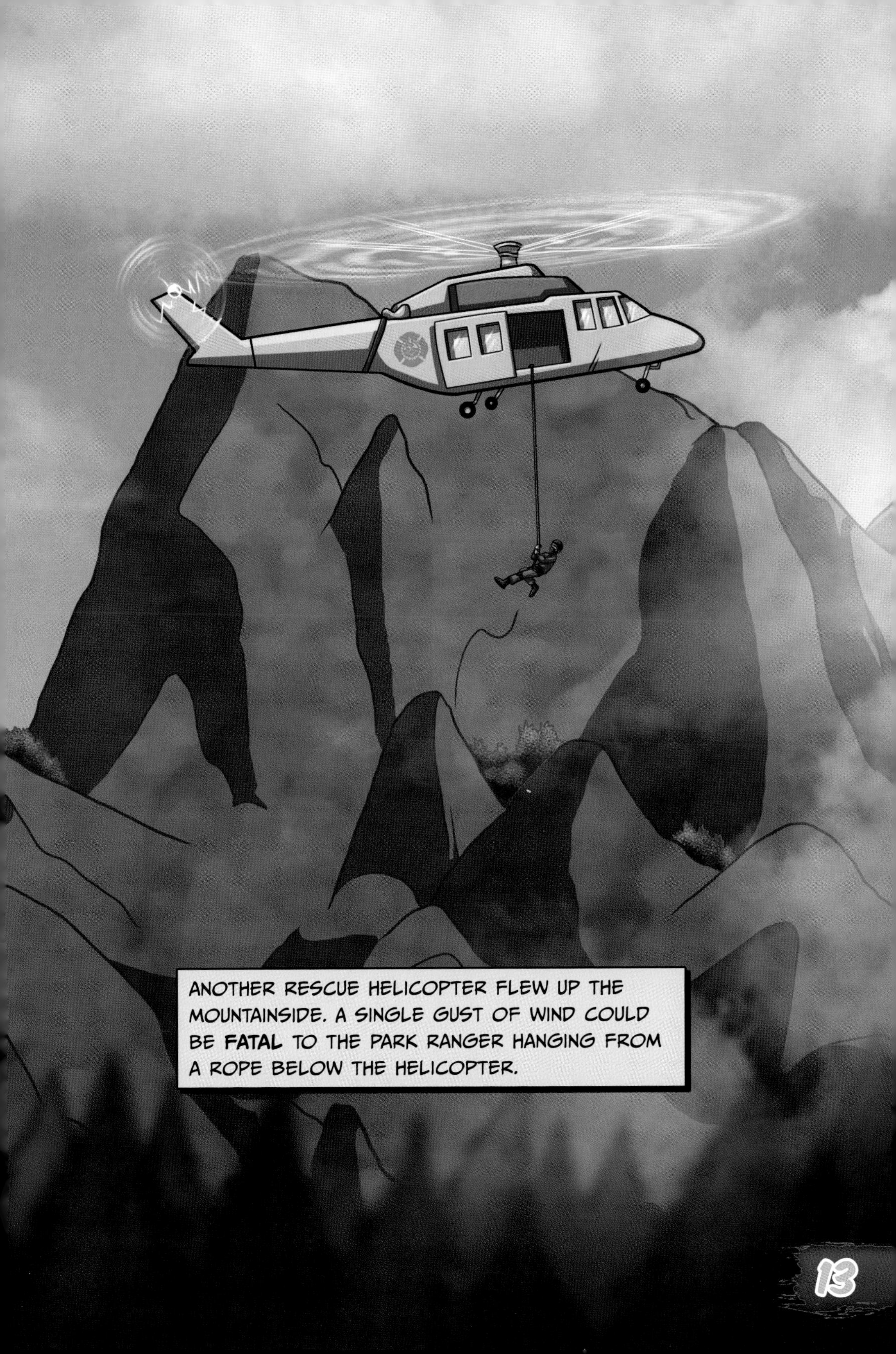
ANOTHER RESCUE HELICOPTER FLEW UP THE MOUNTAINSIDE. A SINGLE GUST OF WIND COULD BE **FATAL** TO THE PARK RANGER HANGING FROM A ROPE BELOW THE HELICOPTER.

Chapter 3

LUCKY TO BE ALIVE

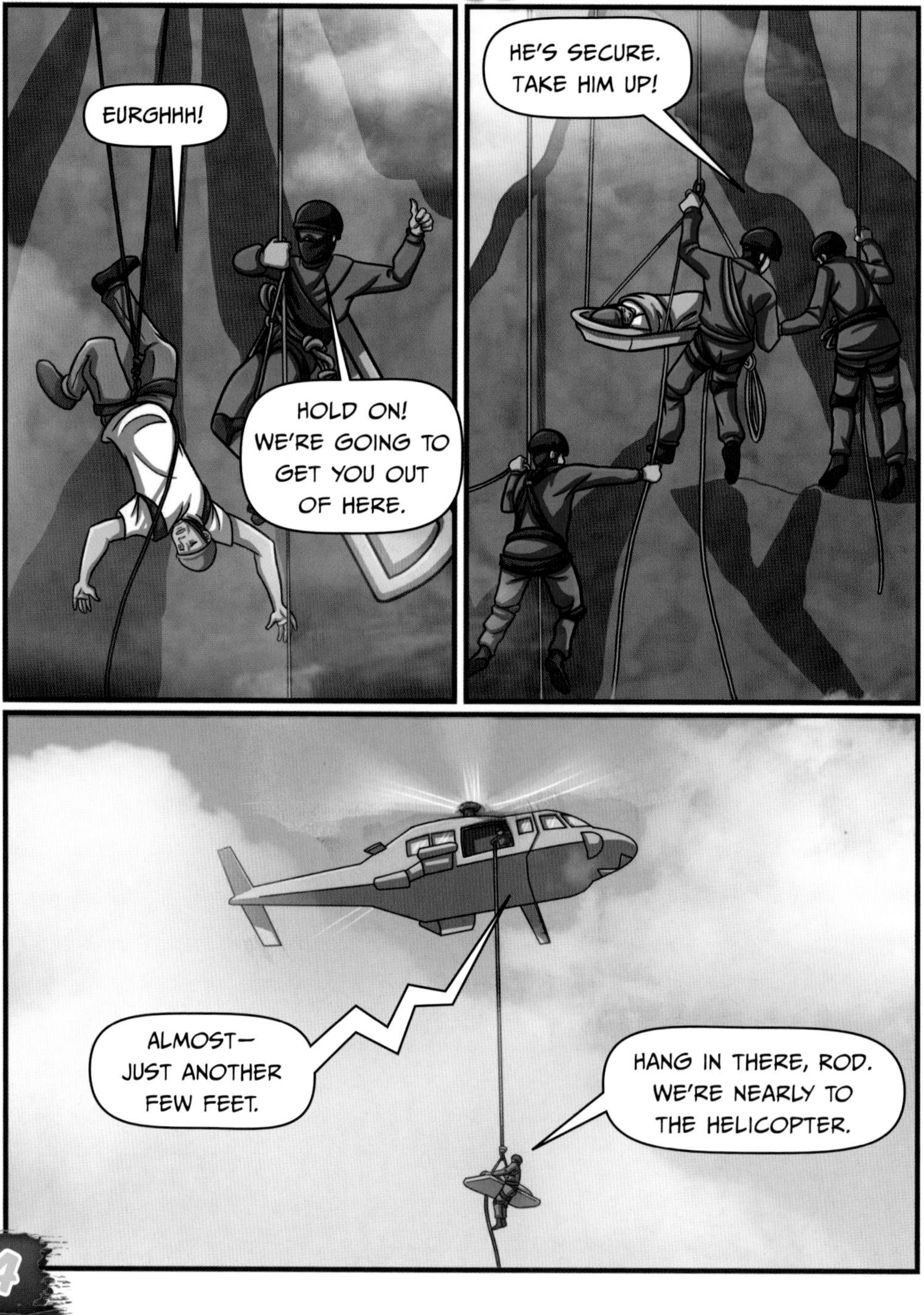
EURGHHH!
HOLD ON! WE'RE GOING TO GET YOU OUT OF HERE.
HE'S SECURE. TAKE HIM UP!
ALMOST— JUST ANOTHER FEW FEET.
HANG IN THERE, ROD. WE'RE NEARLY TO THE HELICOPTER.

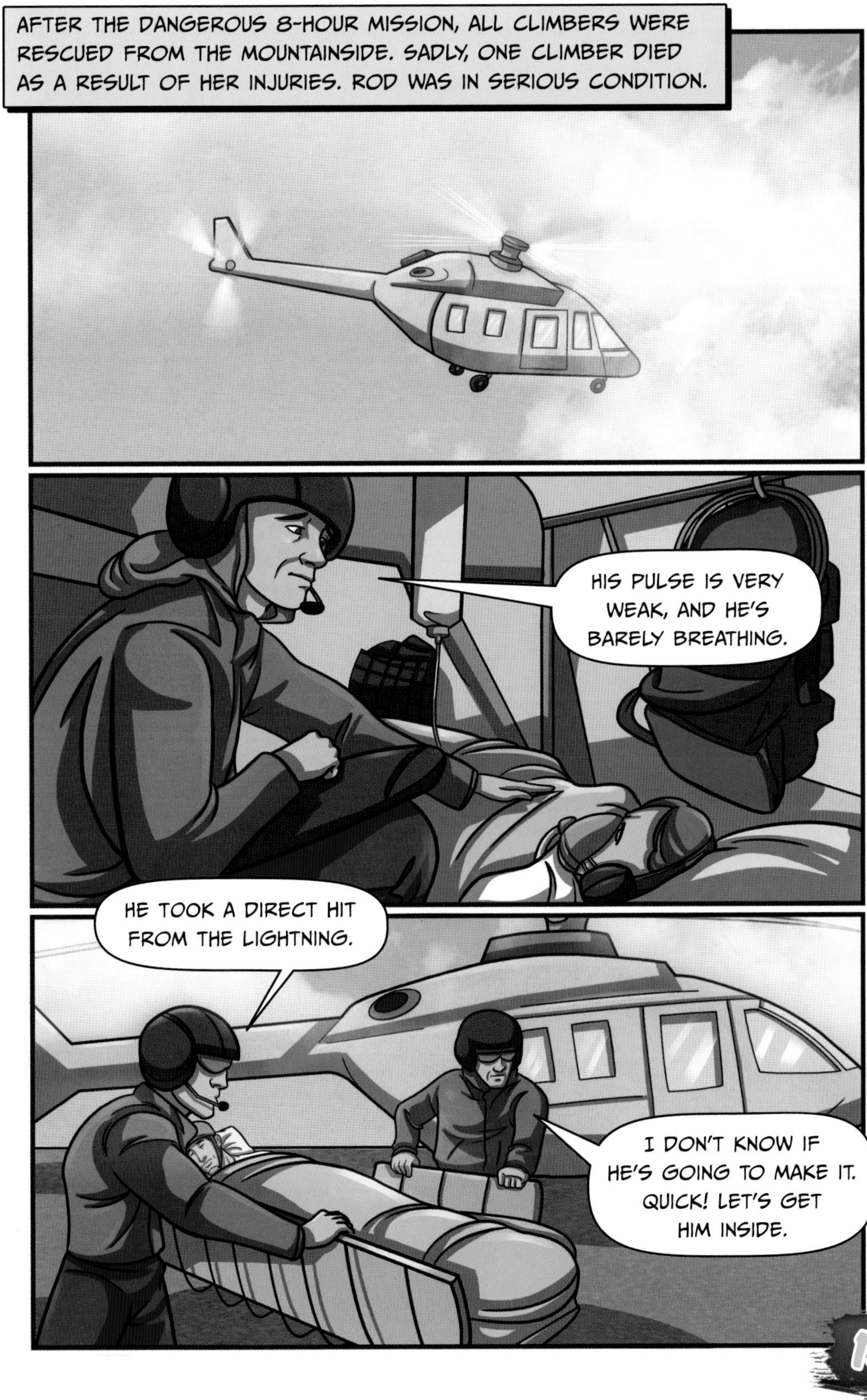
AFTER THE DANGEROUS 8-HOUR MISSION, ALL CLIMBERS WERE RESCUED FROM THE MOUNTAINSIDE. SADLY, ONE CLIMBER DIED AS A RESULT OF HER INJURIES. ROD WAS IN SERIOUS CONDITION.
HIS PULSE IS VERY WEAK, AND HE'S BARELY BREATHING.
HE TOOK A DIRECT HIT FROM THE LIGHTNING.
I DON'T KNOW IF HE'S GOING TO MAKE IT. QUICK! LET'S GET HIM INSIDE.

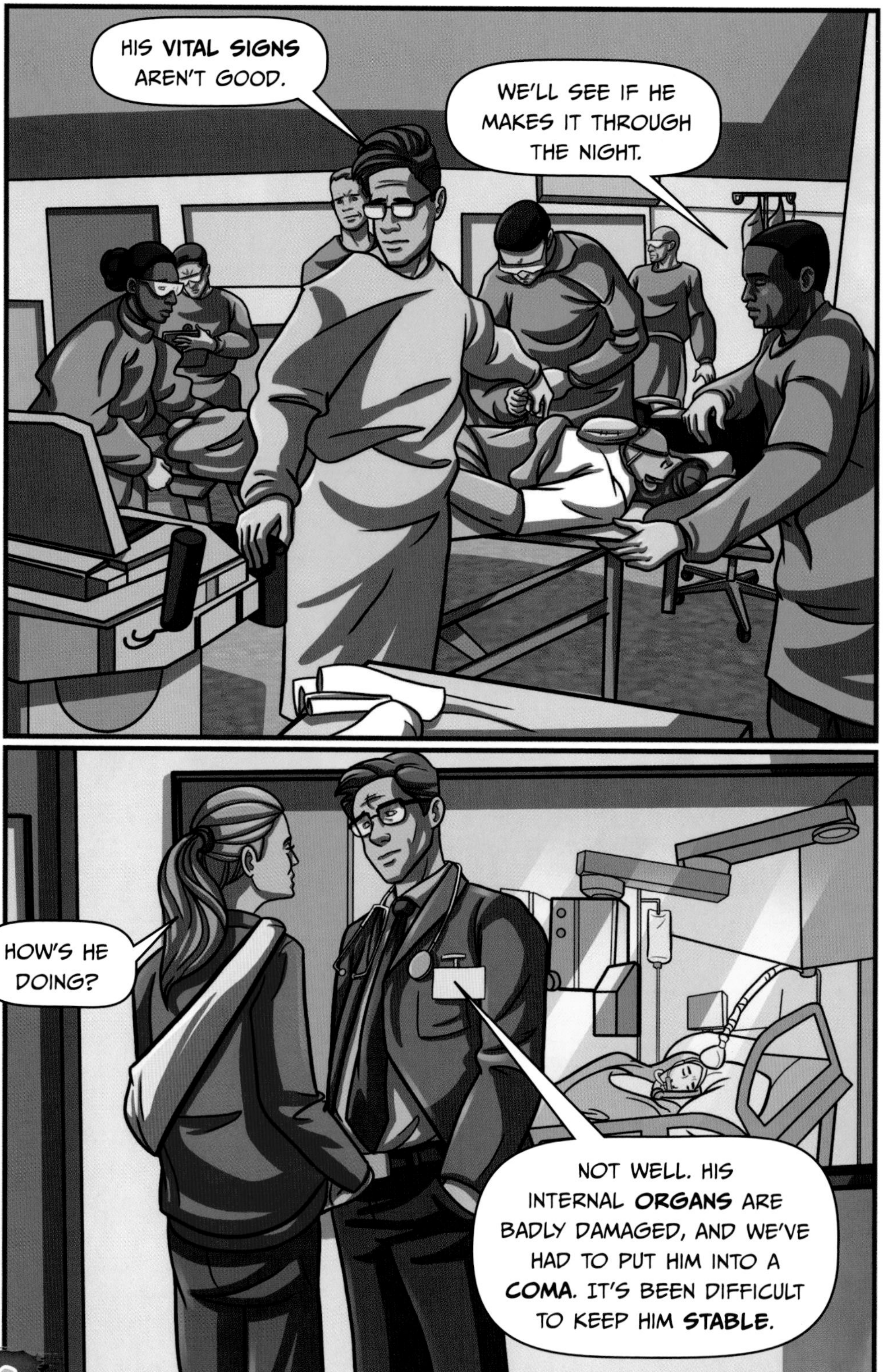

HIS VITAL SIGNS AREN'T GOOD.
WE'LL SEE IF HE MAKES IT THROUGH THE NIGHT.
HOW'S HE DOING?
NOT WELL. HIS INTERNAL ORGANS ARE BADLY DAMAGED, AND WE'VE HAD TO PUT HIM INTO A COMA. IT'S BEEN DIFFICULT TO KEEP HIM STABLE.

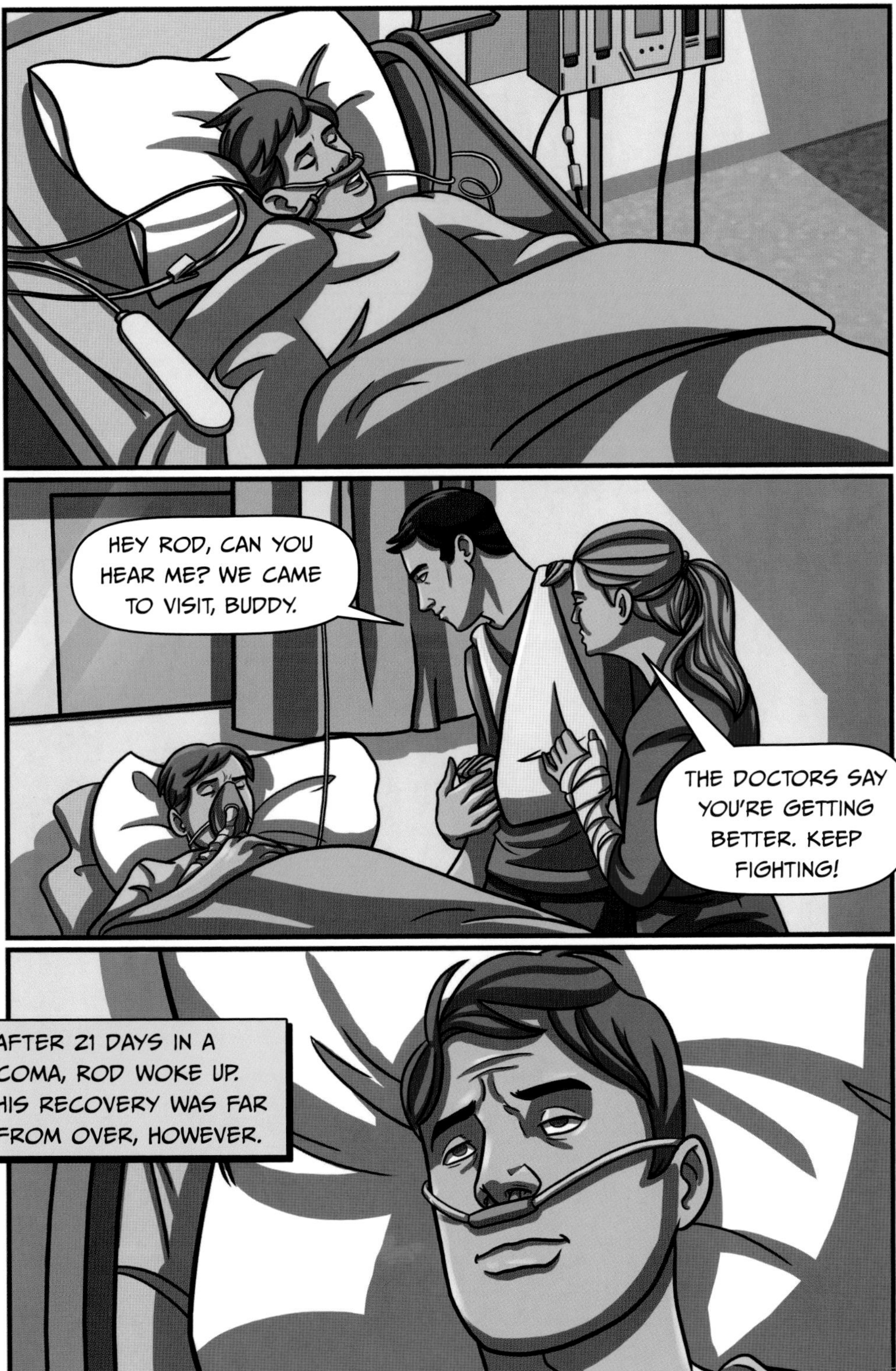
HEY ROD, CAN YOU HEAR ME? WE CAME TO VISIT, BUDDY.
THE DOCTORS SAY YOU'RE GETTING BETTER. KEEP FIGHTING!
AFTER 21 DAYS IN A COMA, ROD WOKE UP. HIS RECOVERY WAS FAR FROM OVER, HOWEVER.

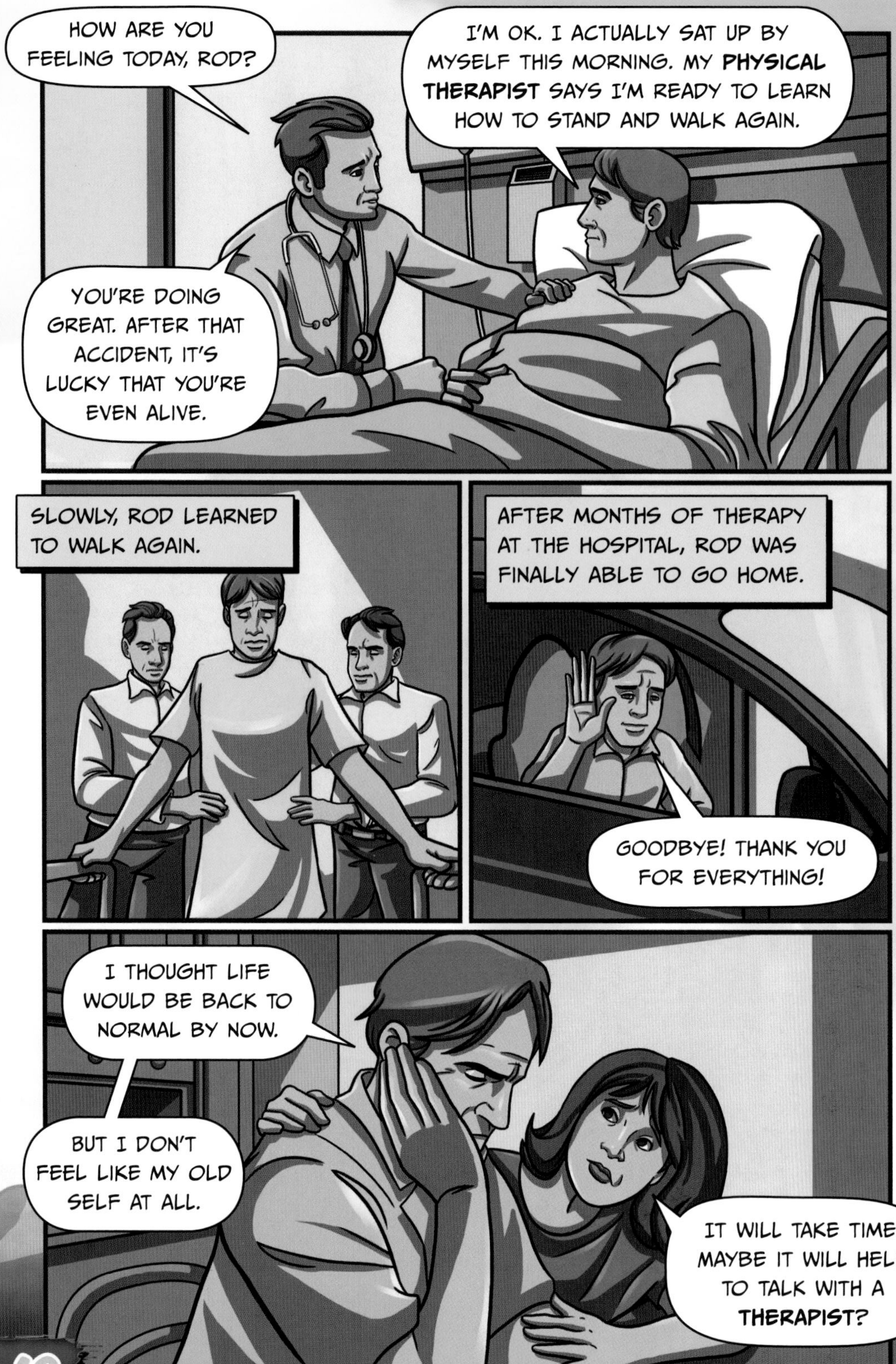
HOW ARE YOU FEELING TODAY, ROD?
I'M OK. I ACTUALLY SAT UP BY MYSELF THIS MORNING. MY **PHYSICAL THERAPIST** SAYS I'M READY TO LEARN HOW TO STAND AND WALK AGAIN.
YOU'RE DOING GREAT. AFTER THAT ACCIDENT, IT'S LUCKY THAT YOU'RE EVEN ALIVE.
SLOWLY, ROD LEARNED TO WALK AGAIN.
AFTER MONTHS OF THERAPY AT THE HOSPITAL, ROD WAS FINALLY ABLE TO GO HOME.
GOODBYE! THANK YOU FOR EVERYTHING!
I THOUGHT LIFE WOULD BE BACK TO NORMAL BY NOW.
BUT I DON'T FEEL LIKE MY OLD SELF AT ALL.
IT WILL TAKE TIME. MAYBE IT WILL HELP TO TALK WITH A **THERAPIST**?

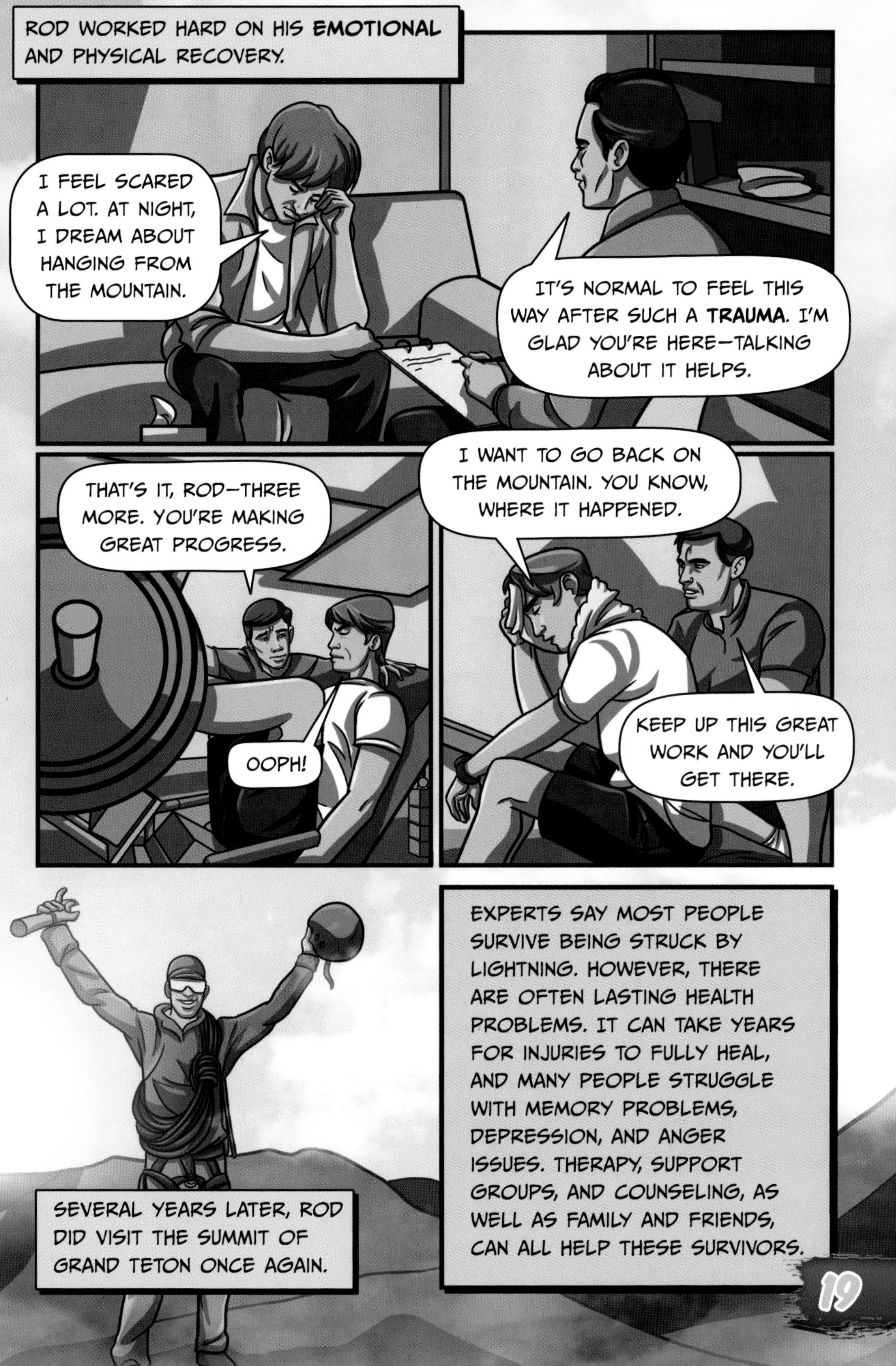
ROD WORKED HARD ON HIS **EMOTIONAL** AND PHYSICAL RECOVERY.
I FEEL SCARED A LOT. AT NIGHT, I DREAM ABOUT HANGING FROM THE MOUNTAIN.
IT'S NORMAL TO FEEL THIS WAY AFTER SUCH A **TRAUMA**. I'M GLAD YOU'RE HERE—TALKING ABOUT IT HELPS.
THAT'S IT, ROD—THREE MORE. YOU'RE MAKING GREAT PROGRESS.
OOPH!
I WANT TO GO BACK ON THE MOUNTAIN. YOU KNOW, WHERE IT HAPPENED.
KEEP UP THIS GREAT WORK AND YOU'LL GET THERE.
SEVERAL YEARS LATER, ROD DID VISIT THE SUMMIT OF GRAND TETON ONCE AGAIN.
EXPERTS SAY MOST PEOPLE SURVIVE BEING STRUCK BY LIGHTNING. HOWEVER, THERE ARE OFTEN LASTING HEALTH PROBLEMS. IT CAN TAKE YEARS FOR INJURIES TO FULLY HEAL, AND MANY PEOPLE STRUGGLE WITH MEMORY PROBLEMS, DEPRESSION, AND ANGER ISSUES. THERAPY, SUPPORT GROUPS, AND COUNSELING, AS WELL AS FAMILY AND FRIENDS, CAN ALL HELP THESE SURVIVORS.

WHAT IS LIGHTNING?

Lightning is a bolt of electricity that jumps from a cloud to the ground or from one cloud to another. But how does lightning form?

Inside clouds high in the sky, tiny pieces of ice rub together. This rubbing creates **electrical charges**. Movement of the air causes the lower part of the cloud to become negatively charged. When the difference between the negative charges in the cloud and positive charges on the ground becomes big enough, a huge spark of electricity jumps to the ground. This is a lightning strike.

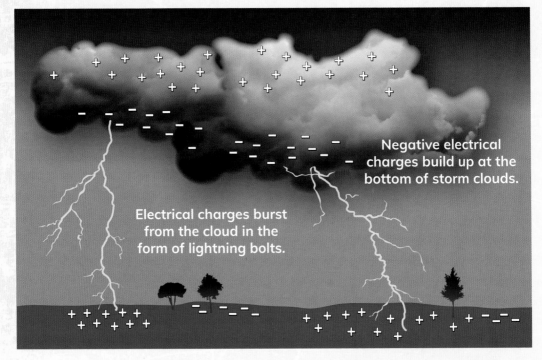

Negative electrical charges build up at the bottom of storm clouds.

Electrical charges burst from the cloud in the form of lightning bolts.

⊕ positive electrical charges
⊖ negative electrical charges

BOLTS OF LIGHTNING ARE USUALLY 1 TO 2 INCHES (2.5 TO 5 CM) WIDE AND CAN BE MORE THAN 20 MILES (32 KM) LONG.

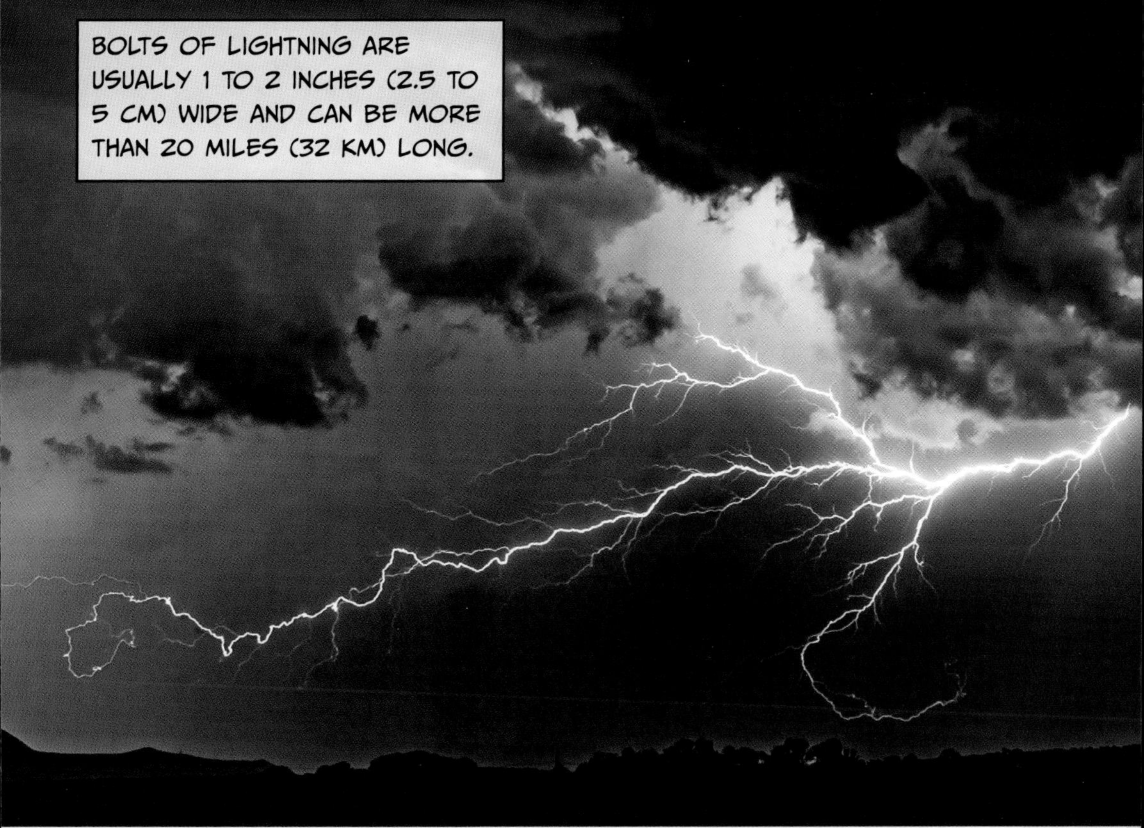

Thunder is the sound made by lightning. A bolt of lightning superheats the air around it, forcing the air to expand very quickly. This makes the sound of thunder. Lightning and thunder occur at the same time. However, we see the lightning before hearing the thunder because light travels faster than sound.

YOU HEAR THUNDER AND SEE LIGHTNING AT THE SAME TIME ONLY IF THE BOLT OF LIGHTNING IS DIRECTLY OVERHEAD.

KEEP SAFE

Here are some lightning safety tips.

- ☑ Check weather reports before going outside during the times of the year when thunderstorms are possible.

- ☑ Stay inside during a thunderstorm. Wait until 30 minutes after the last sound of thunder before going outside.

- ☑ If you are caught outside during a thunderstorm, find a solid building or car to wait in until the storm passes. Don't seek shelter beneath a tree. Lightning is attracted to the highest point, and you could be injured if the tree is struck.

- ☑ If there is no shelter, crouch down low with as little of your body touching the ground as possible.

- ☑ Avoid bodies of water, such as lakes or swimming pools, during a thunderstorm—electricity can easily travel through water.

- ☑ During a thunderstorm, do not use electrical equipment that is plugged into a wall socket.

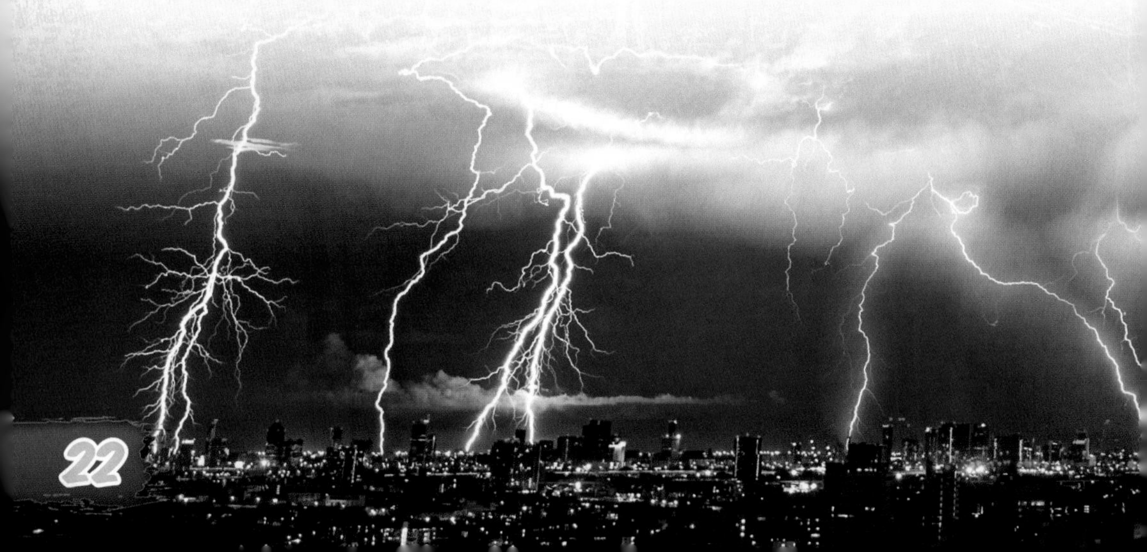

GLOSSARY

coma a state of being unconscious for a long time

electrical charges positive or negative charges that can build up on an object. Electricity is the movement of negative charges.

emotional having to do with someone's emotions or feelings

fatal causing death

organs body parts such as the heart and lungs

paralyzed caused to be unable to move

park rangers people who take care of parks and forests and work to keep visitors safe

physical therapist someone trained to help patients with an illness, disability, or injury through movement and exercise

stable not becoming worse

summit the highest point of a mountain or hill

therapist a person trained to help with feelings and emotions

trauma a very upsetting experience

unconscious not awake or aware of the surroundings

vital signs measurements of a person's body functions, such as how fast the heart is beating

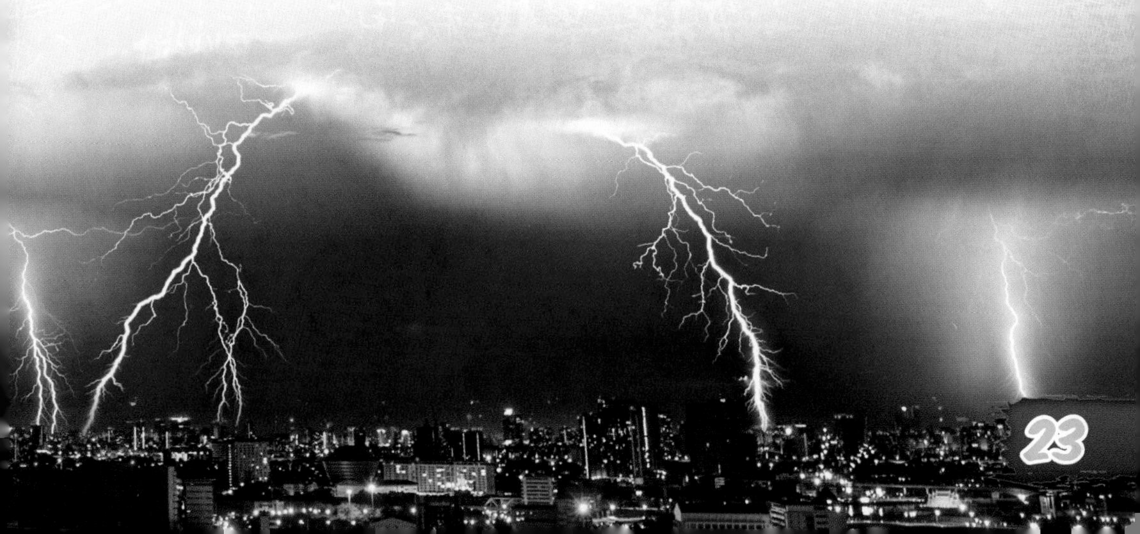

INDEX

READ MORE

Johanson, Paula. *Lightning and Thunder (Nature's Mysteries).* New York: Britannica Educational Publishing (2019).

London, Martha. *Thunderstorms (Extreme Weather).* Minneapolis: Pop! (2020).

McAuliffe, Bill. *Thunderstorms (X-Books: Weather).* Mankato, MN: Creative Education (2018).

LEARN MORE ONLINE

1. Go to **www.factsurfer.com**

2. Enter **"Lightning Survivor"** into the search box.

3. Click on the cover of this book to see a list of websites.